KABALEVSKY

35 EASY PIECES
Opus 89

Edited by Richard Walters

Fingerings are by the composer, except
those in parentheses are editorial additions.

On the cover:
Murnau, Burggrabenstrasse 1 (1908)
by Wassily Kandinsky (1866–1944)

ISBN 978-1-4950-5820-2

G. SCHIRMER, Inc.

DISTRIBUTED BY

7777 W. BLUEMOUND RD. P.O. BOX 13819 MILWAUKEE, WI 53213

www.musicsalesclassical.com
www.halleonard.com

CONTENTS

BIOGRAPHY

Dmitri Kabalevsky (1904–1987)

"Art shapes the man, his heart and mind, his feelings and convictions—the whole of his spiritual world. More than that art influences the development of society" —Dmitri Kabalevsky

Kabalevsky was born in St. Petersburg the son of a mathematician. Dmitri not only learned to play the piano, but also was a competent poet and painter as well. Facing financial difficulties, the family moved to Moscow following the October Revolution of 1917. Economic conditions in Russia were dire following World War I. In the ensuing political upheaval, work was hard to find. The Kabalevskys struggled as part of the working poor. Dmitri assisted in bringing in income, beginning to give piano lessons at 15 and playing for silent films at the theatre. He also held odd jobs, including delivering mail and drawing placards for shop windows.

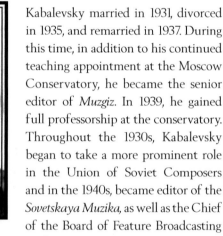

In 1918, Kabalevsky began studying piano and art at the Scriabin Institute. His father wanted him to focus on economics and become a mathematician, but music quickly won the young boy's passions. He soon began teaching at the institute. Kabalevsky enrolled at the Moscow Conservatory in 1925, studying composition and piano.

At the conservatory Kabalevsky joined two musical groups. The Proizvodstvennyi Kollektiv was a conservative, pro-Lenin organization. The Association of Contemporary Musicians was a progressive, avant-garde group. Hardly ten years after the Revolution and the uncertainty of political stability, Kabalevsky deliberately formed relationships with both political camps. This diplomacy would make him one of the most powerful musical voices in the USSR.

Kabalevsky graduated from the conservatory in 1930 and began lecturing there soon after. In 1932, when the Communist Party dissolved all music organizations and created the Union of Soviet Composers, Kabalevsky stepped up as a founding member, using his ties with the more conservative Proizvodstvennyi Kollektiv to demonstrate his commitment to traditional Russian values and the Russian people. He became a writer for the magazine *Muzgiz* and for *Moscow Radio*. These platforms allowed him to endorse Russian music that was "for the people" and condemn the music that was overly "formalist," a catch-all phrase used by Communist leaders to identify art intended for the "intellectual connoisseurs or sophisticated esoterics," ideas the Communists lifted almost directly from Tolstoy's *What is Art?*

Kabalevsky married in 1931, divorced in 1935, and remarried in 1937. During this time, in addition to his continued teaching appointment at the Moscow Conservatory, he became the senior editor of *Muzgiz*. In 1939, he gained full professorship at the conservatory. Throughout the 1930s, Kabalevsky began to take a more prominent role in the Union of Soviet Composers and in the 1940s, became editor of the *Sovetskaya Muzika*, as well as the Chief of the Board of Feature Broadcasting on *Moscow Radio* after joining the Communist Party. The Soviet government considered him important enough to be evacuated during World War II to Sverdlovsk (now Yekaterinburg) as Hitler's army drew closer to Moscow.

Following World War II, the Conference of Musicians at the Central Committee of the All-Union Communist Party was held in 1948 to outline a policy known as Socialist Realism, the official name of Marxist art and aesthetic theory. The policy asked artists to create art that is "comprehensible to the masses, and inspires the people with admiration for the dignity of the working man and his task of building Communism."[1] The conference and ensuing policy spawned widespread questioning of anyone whose music was not politically correct. There were interrogations and threats to those who would not change their style to serve the party. Somehow Kabalevsky managed to get his name removed from the list of potentially "harmful" composers. He is the only prominent Russian composer of the time to avoid interrogation.

Kabalevsky published just over 100 pieces and wrote far more during his life. Most famous today are his suite *The Comedians*, his violin concerto, and several piano collections. The style is always conservative, approachable, and clear, yet quirky, inventive, and light-hearted. Kabalevsky's music demonstrates a master composer capable of disciplined and limited use of material based on a few fundamentals, like a painter that deliberately uses a limited palate of colors.

Beginning in the 1950s until his death, Kabalevsky wrote little music. Instead, he became heavily involved in national and international pedagogical organizations. From 1952 until his death he served on the board of the Union of Soviet Composers of the USSR; in 1953 he became a member of the Soviet Committee for the Defense of Peace; in 1954, USSR Ministry of Culture; in 1955, World Peace Council; in 1961, United Nations Educational, Scientific and Cultural Organization International Music Council, Council of Directors of the International Society for Music Education. Later, he became a member of the Committee for Lenin Prizes for Literature and Art, the Head of the Council on Aesthetic Education, a deputy to the USSR Supreme Council, Honorary President of the Academy of Pedagogical Sciences in the USSR, and Honorary President of the International Society of Music Education.

During much of this time, Kabalevsky also gave lectures on radio, television, and at various functions in many different countries on music appreciation, pedagogy, and aesthetics.

Perhaps Kabalevsky's most enduring contribution to Soviet music education was his work with the Laboratory of Musical Education in the 1970s. He succeeded in compiling specific lesson plans to be implemented in all Soviet classrooms. It became a complete syllabus (texts, recordings, and detailed outlines of each lesson) for all music education in the country. He then went into the primary schools of Moscow to implement this system. The program focused on political indoctrination, moral education, and character training at its base. Eventually Kabalevsky retired from the conservatory and dedicated his full attention to the education of children in primary schools. He stated in 1974, "when I decided it was time to sum up my work in this [music education] field, I discovered that it was not the summing up, but the beginning of a new stage. I realized that all I had done was merely preparation for going into general schools not merely as a composer or lecturer, but as an ordinary teacher of music."[2]

Up to the last moments of his life Kabalevsky was furthering music education and peaceful relations between all people of all cultures. He died of a heart attack at a conference at which he was to deliver a lecture on the disarmament of world powers of their nuclear weapons.

In Frank Callaway's eulogy given a few days later, he summed up the great influence of the composer: "Kabalevsky believed and demonstrated that music cultivates the artistic tastes and the creative imagination of children, as well as their love of life, of people, of nature, of motherland, and fosters their interest in, and friendships toward, peoples of all nations."[3]

[1] David Lawrence Forrest, *The Educational Theory of Dmitri Kabalevsky in Relation to His Piano Music for Children* (Ph.D. diss., University of Melbourne. 1996), 87.

[2] ibid., 36.

[3] ibid., 40.

INTRODUCTION TO KABALEVSKY'S MUSIC

"We live in a difficult—interesting but difficult—epoch, but still life is wonderful. Great art can only come from love for life, love for man. Art must serve society, the people must understand it. The love of man must be there." —Dmitri Kabalevsky.[1]

In his book *Music and Education: A Composer Writes About Musical Education*, Kabalevsky several times cites the quotation by Maxim Gorki that books for children should be "the same as for adults, only better."[2] This quotation is the guiding principle behind all of Kabalevsky's music for children. He did not want to compose simplified or dumbed-down adult art, but good art for children. This flowed very naturally out of his educational theories, that of teaching musical literacy rather than musical grammar, instructing how to listen to music, define shapes and structures, not just how to read or how to identify elements of music.

Building an educational framework, Kabalevsky's book *A Story of Three Whales and Many Other Things* identifies three archetypes as basic musical forms from which all other larger forms are generated and most accessible to children: song, dance, and march. The archetypes (or whales) become the bridges upon which children may enter the world of music. Nearly all of Kabalevsky's music for children can be understood as fitting into one of these categories.

Kabalevsky believed that "no piece of music, however short and modest, should pass by a child without touching his mind and heart."[3] And it is easy to hear in his pedagogical works that he was focusing on developing a real musical understanding in children rather than just getting them to practice or learn scales.

Kabalevsky composed 253 pieces during his lifetime. There are 26 sonatas, sets or suites of piano music, from concert level works for advanced players to 153 pieces specifically written for progressing piano students. It is no wonder he has remained such a popular choice among piano teachers.

[1] in an interview with *The New York Times*, October 27, 1957 "Optimistic Russian: Kabalevsky, in Speaking of His Fourth Symphony, Reveals Attitude to Life" (quoted in Forrest, 103).

[2] Dmitri Kabalevsky, *Music and Education: A Composer Writes About Musical Education* (London: Jessica Kingsley Publishers, 1988), 120.

[3] David Lawrence Forrest, *The Educational Theory of Dmitri Kabalevsky in Relation to His Piano Music for Children* (Ph.D. diss., University of Melbourne. 1996), 143.

References

Daragan, Dina Grigor'yevna. "Kabalevsky, Dmitry Borisovich," *The New Grove Dictionary of Music and Musicians*. ed. S. Sadie and J. Tyrrell. London: Macmillan. 2001.

Forrest, David Lawrence. *The Educational Theory of Dmitri Kabalevsky in Relation to His Piano Music for Children*. (Ph.D. diss., University of Melbourne. 1996).

Kabalevsky, Dimitri. *Music and Education: A Composer Writes About Musical Education*. London: Jessica Kingsley Publishers, 1988.

Krebs, Stanley Dale. *Soviet Composers and the Development of Soviet Music*. New York: W. W. Norton & Company, 1970.

Maes Francis. trans. Arnold J. and Erica Pomerans. *A History of Russian Music: From Kamarinskaya to Babi Yar*. Berkley: University of California Press, 2002.

—Richard Walters, editor
and Joshua Parman, assistant editor

35 EASY PIECES
OP. 89

Kabalevsky's last set of pedagogical piano pieces for students, *35 Easy Pieces*, Op. 89, was composed between 1972 and 1974, when the composer was in his late sixties. This was after he had accumulated decades of experiences with young musicians, and after he had attained a revered position as the cultural leader of music education in the USSR. These were also his last compositions for piano. (*Lyric Melodies,* Op. 93a, were written before Op. 89.) After 1974 Kabalevsky only wrote only approximately five more compositions, which were songs or small choral pieces.

In Kabalevsky's output for piano, *35 Easy Pieces* mostly closely resembles *24 Pieces for Children*, Op. 39, which was composed thirty years earlier. Both sets begin at approximately the same level, and progress to similar levels by the end. Both are comprised of exquisite miniatures composed to teach technical as well as musical progress at the piano. Articulation as an integral and organic part of composition is emphasized from the first piece. In comparing both sets it could perhaps be said that the pieces of Opus 89 are even more sharply and economically composed, with music created of the smallest and most essential elements. Yet for reasons that are not easy to discern, at

this writing *35 Easy Pieces,* Op. 89, is less well-known than *24 Pieces for Children*, Op. 39. There is nothing about the quality of the music that would justify that. Both sets are of top-notch, attractive and imaginative composition throughout.

Sometimes it's easy to discern what Kabalevsky intends to teach the student in a specific piece. Numbers 1–3 of Opus 89 emphasize a legato touch. Number 4 introduces independence of the hands in articulation, another theme that recurs many times, such as in numbers 13, 15, 19, 20, 27, 29, 31 and 34. Crossing of hands comes in as early as the first piece, and is brought back several times: numbers 6, 10, 17 and 21. A prominent melody in one hand with accompaniment in the other hand is taught in numbers 5, 19, 20, 29 and 33. Staccato is featured in numbers 4, 7, 8, and then regularly. Kabalevsky teaches the student enharmonic note spellings in number 12, "The Shrew." Double thirds come in with "Morning Song," number 14; sixteenth notes are introduced in number 18, "On the Ice"; irregular meter is taught in number 19; and dotted eighth notes are highlighted beginning in number 22. Many other pedagogical concepts appear throughout the compositions.

PRACTICE AND PERFORMANCE TIPS

First Piece, Op. 89, No. 1
Practice and Performance Tips
- Make a graceful phrase in the right hand, and answer it with a graceful phrase in the left hand.
- Smoothly pass the phrase from the right to the left hand in measures 9–10 and 11–12.
- Note the progression from *p* to *mf* and back to *p* in this brief piece.
- Gently and gracefully cross the left hand over for the final note.
- Use no pedal at all.

First Etude, Op. 89, No. 2
Practice and Performance Tips
- Though relatively simple, this etude is musically challenging.
- The composer asks the player to create a four-measure phrase moving from hand to hand.
- The music also puts the hands close together in spots, creating additional challenges.
- Though marked *mf*, Kabalevsky has also indicated *Tranquillo*; the music needs a gentle flow.
- Do not take this etude too quickly.
- Create the legato and phrase completely with the fingers.
- Use no pedal at all.

Quiet Song, Op. 89, No. 3
Practice and Performance Tips
- The right hand changes position in measure 4, then again in measures 7, 11 and 14.
- The left hand changes position in measures 6 and 13.
- Take special note of the composer's phrase markings, and smoothly pass the phrase from the right to the left hand.
- Practice at *mf* until you are confident, then begin practicing at *p*. Note the title of the piece!
- *Cantabile* means a singing tone, which implies smooth playing.
- Use no pedal at all.

At Recess, Op. 89, No. 4
Practice and Performance Tips
- The piece is comprised of three elements: two-note slurs, staccato notes, and four-note phrases.
- Each element must be precisely played to create the playful spirit of "At Recess."

- Make certain to smoothly move from right hand to left hand in measures 8 and 15.
- Though played *f*, this piece still requires a buoyant touch.
- Practice slowly with both hands together.
- Use no pedal at all.

First Waltz, Op. 89, No. 5
Practice and Performance Tips
- The melody is in the left hand throughout.
- Note that Kabalevsky has added tenuto stress marks to the melody.
- The right hand is accompaniment, and should be played slightly softer than the left hand.
- Practice each hand separately at first.
- Be sure to play a legato phrase in the left hand as marked, measures 5–8 and 9–12.
- Kabalevsky's tempo of *Non allegro* warns you not to play this rather sad piece too quickly.
- Use no pedal at all.

The Jumping Champion, Op. 89, No. 6
Practice and Performance Tips
- Kabalevsky is teaching hand-crossing, radical shifts in hand position, and ledger lines in "The Jumping Champion."
- The composer asks for no subtly here; it is *f* throughout and all notes are *marcato*.
- A tricky spot is the interruption of the pattern in measure 9.
- Some students may need to write the note names next to the notes high above the staff.
- The challenges may be daunting to some at first, but after practice the piece is fun to play.

Light and Shadow, Op. 89, No. 7
Practice and Performance Tips
- The "light" is the loud music; the "shadow" is the soft music.
- Notice the contrast between the staccato markings and those notes without staccato.
- Be careful not to play all notes staccato.
- First practice hands separately, slowly.
- Then practice hands together, slowly.
- Retain the composed articulation in your practice, no matter what tempo.
- Use no pedal at all.

Little Hedgehog, Op. 89, No. 8

Practice and Performance Tips

- Notice that every note of the piece is played staccato, with the final three notes also accented.
- Kabalevsky has indicated *staccatissimo*, meaning extremely short, crisp staccato.
- Practice right and left hands separately, and initially at a slow tempo.
- The sudden *p* in measure 8 followed by the crescendo creates a fun effect.
- Use no pedal at all.

Song in Octaves, Op. 89, No. 9

Practice and Performance Tips

- Kabalevsky is teaching at least three elements: legato fingers, phrase and ledger lines.
- The crescendo in measure 2 leads to a stress on the downbeat of measure 3, creating a natural phrase.
- The second phrase, beginning in measure 4, culminates in something akin to *mf* in measure 6.
- The *p* in measure 7 is a sudden change, *subito*.
- Because the hands are playing in octaves, it's easy to introduce the high notes on ledger lines in the left hand.
- The legato should be accomplished through the fingers; use no pedal.

Playful One, Op. 89, No. 10

Practice and Performance Tips

- Gracefully cross the left hand over the right hand in measures 4, 6, 10 and 12.
- Practice hands together, first at a slow tempo.
- Notice the two and three note slurs that Kabalevsky has composed.
- Accurately playing the slurs as composed will make the piece "playful."
- Use no pedal at all.

Crybaby, Op. 89, No. 11

Practice and Performance Tips

- This unusual piece focuses on two note slurs and exact pedaling.
- Each two note slur, beginning at *p*, has a *diminuendo* from the first to the second note.
- Kabalevsky asks that the sustaining pedal be released exactly on the eighth note, creating a rest at the end of each measure.
- The left hand crosses the right briefly in measure 12.

The Shrew, Op. 89, No. 12

Practice and Performance Tips

- Kabalevsky is teaching the student about enharmonic spelling of notes in this piece.
- Enharmonics means that the same note is notated different ways. For instance, B-flat or A-sharp.
- Left and right hands play the same notes in octaves throughout.
- Most measures are comprised of an accented half note slurred to a short eighth note.
- Learn and accomplish the articulation with the fingers only before using the pedaling Kabalevsky has composed.
- When using the pedaling, be sure to release exactly as you play the eighth note on beat 3.
- This is a character piece, in this case a portrait of a strident, hot tempered woman (a shrew).

Soothing Song, Op. 89, No. 13

Practice and Performance Tips

- In this haunting melody Kabalevsky teaches using both hands to make one phrase.
- The phrase should pass from the right hand to the left hand imperceptibly and smoothly.
- Notice the slight emphasis on the longer notes in the left hand at the end of the phrase in measures 2, 4, 10 and 12.
- Use no pedal.

Morning Song, Op. 89, No. 14

Practice and Performance Tips

- Kabalevsky introduces the student to parallel thirds in each hand in this tricky little piece.
- The composer's fingering, used in this edition, is minimal, but sets the hand position.
- In measure 3 it is implied that the fingering begins with 3 and 1 in the right hand, and 3 and 5 in the left hand.
- For most students it will take some practice for the thirds to feel comfortable.
- Notice the phrase markings, which ask for smooth, legato playing.
- The music swells in volume in measures 8–11 before the unexpected ending.
- Use no pedal.

Trumpet and Echo, Op. 89, No. 15

Practice and Performance Tips

- The right hand is the trumpet and the left hand is the echo.
- The right hand plays *f*, with each note articulated and accented.
- In contrast, the left hand plays softly and legato, moving from note to note smoothly.
- The composer's marking *marcato* refers to the right hand only.
- Practice hands together, first at a slow tempo.
- Use no pedal at all.

Evening Song, Op. 89, No. 16

Practice and Performance Tips

- Practice first hands together slowly.
- Note that the composer passes the legato phrase from the right hand to the left hand.
- When the dynamic moves to **mf**, the texture changes to short two-note phrases in the right hand.
- Note the stressed notes in measures 13–14, which will help make the two-note phrases.
- A slight *ritard.* in the final measure is possible, leading to the final note.
- *Andante cantabile* indicates careful attention to the smooth, flowing phrase throughout.
- Use no pedal at all.

Skipping Rope, Op. 89, No. 17

Practice and Performance Tips

- Practice hands together, first at a slow tempo.
- Play staccato throughout, except for the last accented note.
- The trickiest challenge in this piece is hands crossing each other.
- Right hand crosses left hand in measures 3 and 7.
- Left hand crosses right hand in measures 10 and 12.
- The words *accel. poco a poco al fine* mean to accelerate the tempo little by little until the end.
- Use no pedal at all.

On the Ice, Op. 89, No. 18

Practice and Performance Tips

- Each short phrase could be the blade of the skate on the ice.
- The left hand imitates the right hand in the sixteenth note phrase through most of the piece.
- Make sure all sixteenth notes, in either hand, sound even and clear.
- The rhythmic texture changes in measure 7 with the introduction of a sustained, accented note in the right hand and staccato eighth notes in the left hand.
- The transition in measure 7 will likely take some practice.
- Kabalevsky challenges the student in measure 10, when the sixteenth notes are now in descent, by overlapping the right and left hands.
- Measures 10–13 will require special attention for most.
- It is suggested that practice begins at a slow tempo, achieving *Vivo* after the piece is well in the hands.

Little Goat Limping, Op. 89, No. 19

Practice and Performance Tips

- For this piece in 5/4 time signature, the composer has helped by putting in dotted bar lines to divide

the measure into two groups: 3 beats + 2 beats.
- Find the natural lilt in this music in 5/4, with a stronger emphasis on beat 1, followed by a lighter emphasis on beat 4.
- Executing the slurs and accents as Kabalevsky composed them will create the character of the piece.
- We suggest playing beats 3 and 5 in the right hand in measures 1–3 with separation just short of true staccato.
- Notice how the composer decorates the melody a bit when the music from measures 1–4 returns in measures 9–12 with different slurring the second time.
- Use no pedal in this crisply rhythmic piece.

Trumpet and Drum, Op. 89, No. 20

Practice and Performance Tips

- The left hand represents the drum throughout, which should be played *marcato* and very steadily.
- The right hand is the trumpet.
- Accurately play the two note slurs in the right hand.
- Carefully and enthusiastically play the accents as the composers has indicated.
- Even though the piece begins **f**, in measure 13 the composer asks for even more volume.
- Use no pedal at all.

The Little Juggler, Op. 89, No. 21

Practice and Performance Tips

- *Scherzando* means playful, which is the key to this fun piece.
- Just as juggling takes practice and coordination, so will this piece, which deliberately asks for sometimes radical shifts in hand positions.
- Practice should begin at a slow tempo.
- The entire piece is **f**, so no subtly is required. However, an even staccato touch is needed throughout.

March, Op. 89, No. 22

Practice and Performance Tips

- Kabalevsky introduces unusually positioned two note slurs.
- Playing the slurring as composed is essential to the piece.
- Be sure to sustain the half note chords longer than the quarter-note chords.
- Though the composer did not indicate a dynamic, the tempo *Risoluto* (resolutely) implies **mf** to **f**.

Brave Song, Op. 89, No. 23

Practice and Performance Tips

- *Con fuoco* means "with fire."
- Practice should begin slowly before working up to a fiery tempo.

- Dynamics are always relative. Even though Kabalevsky asks for f at the beginning, he later asks for a crescendo and then *più* f (louder). Make sure there is somewhere to go in volume with your beginning dynamic.
- Kabalevsky plays with the relationship of major and minor with the E-sharps and E-naturals in measures 9–12.
- Notice the strong accent on the syncopated left hand note on beat two of measure 17.

The Little Harpist, Op. 89, No. 24
Practice and Performance Tips
- As the title indicates, this music imitates a harp.
- It is crucial to play the composer's phrasing, passing the phrase from hand to hand.
- A traditional technical approach would be to practice slowly, deliberately playing *non legato*, making each sixteenth note very even.
- Follow the above by playing smoothly and elegantly, but attempting to retain the evenness of the sixteenth notes.
- As the music is mastered, the tempo can increase.
- Practice without pedal. Kabalevsky (who often indicated pedaling in his piano music) did not mark any pedaling, a strong clue that he intended this little piece to be played without pedal.

Chastushka, Op. 89, No. 25
Practice and Performance Tips
- A *chastushka* is a short, lighthearted, satirical verse in Russian, similar to a limerick in English.
- Though Kabalevsky has asked for crossing of hands before this point in opus 89, this piece is by far the most challenging so far in this regard in the set.
- Practice will need to begin slowly, increasing speed as the piece is mastered.
- The radical, quick shifts in hand position for the left hand are the biggest challenge.
- Kabalevsky provided no beginning dynamic. We suggest f.
- Crisp and exact execution of the composed dynamics and articulations will create the wit in the music the composer intended.
- Note the very brief pedal the composer wrote, emphasizing each downbeat.

A Merry Game, Op. 89, No. 26
Practice and Performance Tips
- Kabalevsky uses the interval of parallel sixths throughout, until the final measure.
- Essentially, the left hand note harmonizes the right-hand melody.
- Very exact pedaling happens briefly in measures 1–2 and 17–18.
- Except where marked, use no pedal.
- Carefully observe the articulations, whether staccato or slurred notes.
- The changes in articulation create contrasts essential to the music.

Stubborn Little Brother, Op. 89, No. 27
Practice and Performance Tips
- The wit of this adorable piece comes from someone attempting to persuade sweetly, with a blunt response that refuses to comply.
- Through most of the piece (except for measures 18–20) the right hand plays smoothly and the left hand plays with strong *marcato* accents.
- Practice slowly hands together.
- The pedaling is by the composer. Pedal exactly as he wrote it, using pedal nowhere else.
- Be sure to release the pedal cleanly, exactly in the spot the composer indicates.
- Typical of Kabalevsky, the piece has many intricate details of articulation, slurring, dynamics and pedaling, all composed along with the notes.

Buratino's Dance, Op. 89, No. 28
Practice and Performance Tips
- The character Buratino originated in the *commedia dell'arte*, a tradition of stock comic characters who improvised in traveling theatrical troupes. Buratino is also the main character of an Aleksey Nikolayevich Tolstoy's novel *The Golden Key, or The Adventures of Buratino*, which was based on the Italian novel *The Adventures of Pinocchio* by Carlo Collodi.
- Buratino is a wooden puppet or doll. The name is derived from the Italian word *burattino*, which means puppet.
- Imagine the jerky dance of Pinocchio in this piece.
- The two note slur is the motive throughout.
- Kabalevsky challenges the student by hand positions changing frequently.
- Begin practice at a slow tempo, moving to a faster tempo as the music is mastered.

Melody, Op. 89, No. 29
Practice and Performance Tips
- This melancholic piece shifts between minor and major.
- Throughout, the right hand melody is accompanied by thirds in the left hand.
- Pay careful attention to the phrase markings the composer has written for the melody.
- Kabalevsky provided no tempo indication, but his *"tranquillo, cantabile"* implies a relaxed tempo that is not too fast.

- Unlike most of the other works in this volume, Kabalevsky gives a general indication about pedaling: *"tenuto con Ped."* meaning sustained, with pedal.
- Be sure to clear the pedal for the indicated rests in the left hand.

Fighting Song, Op. 89, No. 30

Practice and Performance Tips

- This lively little piece is all about a spritely melody in the right hand, with occasional punctuation added by the left hand.
- Practice the right hand alone, first at a slow tempo.
- Pay careful attention to the slurs, phrasing and articulation Kabalevsky wrote to find the right shape to the melody.
- Note the brief use of the sustaining pedal in measures 6, 8, 14 and 16.

Rabbit Teasing a Bear-Cub, Op. 89, No. 31

Practice and Performance Tips

- The right hand represents the quick movements of the rabbit.
- The left hand represents the slower, less coordinated movements of the bear cub.
- First practice hands alone separately, learning all the details of articulation.
- When putting hands together in practice, retain all the details of articulation mastered in hands alone practice.
- Pay careful attention to the dynamics, which help create the character and scene.
- Measure 9 is where the rabbit is most annoying to the bear.
- In the last line of the music, it's as if the rabbit has gone too far in annoying the bear and is scampering away.
- Performing a character piece such as this needs wit and fun. Let the imagery of the rabbit and bear help you create a colorful performance.
- Use no pedal at all.

Little Hippo Dance, Op. 89, No. 32

Practice and Performance Tips

- The slow, thick music, emphasizing the bass of the piano, conjures the heavy, yet in its own way, playful movement of a baby hippopotamus.
- Kabalevsky intends for the pedal to continue be changed on the half measure throughout. The exception is the next to last measure, where the harmony changes on beat 4. We have suggested a different pedaling for this measure, indicated in the score.
- Kabalevsky is teaching independence of the fingers, with the thumb or fifth finger held down and sustained while the other fingers of the hand are playing a melody.
- The hands play the same notes in octaves throughout.
- At the climax of the piece, measure 15, marked ***ff***, *molto pesante* means very heavy.

Almost a Waltz, Op. 89, No. 33

Practice and Performance Tips

- In the meter changes the composer has indicated how the measure divides.
- 7/4 measures (most of the piece) are a combination of 4 beats + 3 beats, indicated by the dotted bar line.
- 6/4 measures are a combination of 3 beats + 3 beats, indicated by the dotted bar line.
- Because the quarter note stays the same throughout, these meters are not difficult to comprehend.
- Keep the quarter note beat steady throughout, except in the section marked *poco rit.*
- *Cantando* means singing, applied to the right-hand melody, which is to be played gracefully and smoothly.
- Divide the piece into sections for practice. For instance: section 1: measures 1–17; section 2: measures 18–25; section 3: measures 24–38.
- It is very important to release the pedal exactly as indicated.
- The right hand melody should be slightly brought out above the accompaniment in the left hand.
- Do not take this piece too fast, which will destroy the *tranquillo* mood the composer requests.
- A performance of this piece should be graceful and elegant.

Melancholy Rain, Op. 89, No. 34

Practice and Performance Tips

- Independence of the hands is a major element in learning piano. In this piece Kabalevsky asks the left hand to play staccato throughout, while the right hand plays an expressive, smooth melody.
- Practice each hand separately.
- When practicing the left hand, aim for evenness of touch and sound, and steadiness. Keep the staccato tone the same to the end.
- The composer asks for *poco marcato* in measures 11–12, a heavier staccato.
- Note the *marcato* for the left hand, very sharply struck staccato, at measure 22, the climax of the piece.
- The right hand is marked *cantabile*, as if a sung melody. Use the phrasing Kabalevsky has composed in shaping the melody.
- The many dynamic contrasts should be observed, creating drama.

By the Water, Op. 89, No. 35

Practice and Performance Tips

- With *35 Easy Pieces* in progressive order, it is not surprising that the last of the set is the most sophisticated piece.
- The piece asks for musicality and sensitivity, using all Kabalevsky's indications of pedaling, dynamics, and *ritardando* to creative an expressive, moody statement.
- Notice the stress on the first note of the right hand in measures 1–3, implying that the phrase diminuendos after that first note.
- In contrast, notice that the last note of the left hand has the stress in measures 1–3, implying that unlike the right hand, the phrase builds over the phrase.
- The contrasts above should be subtly stated, not exaggerated.
- The two note slur in the right hand in measures 6, 8, and 11–13 are an important musical element.

–Richard Walters, editor

35 EASY PIECES

Dmitri Kabalevsky
Op. 89

1
First Piece

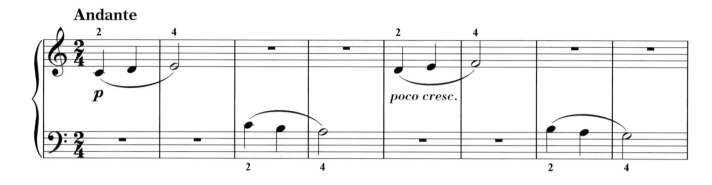

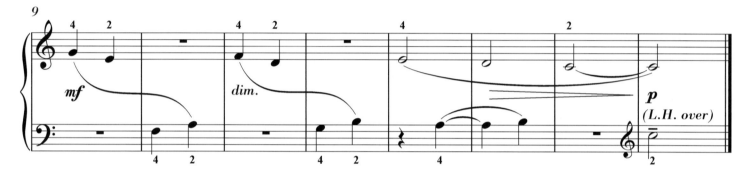

2
First Etude

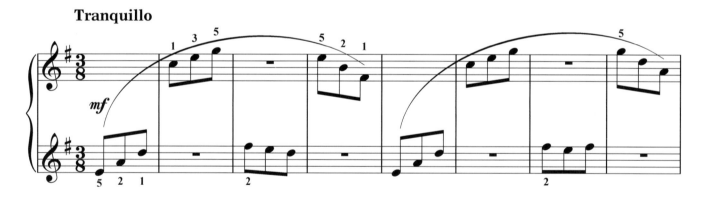

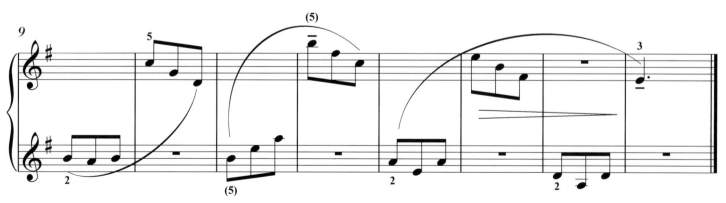

3
Quiet Song

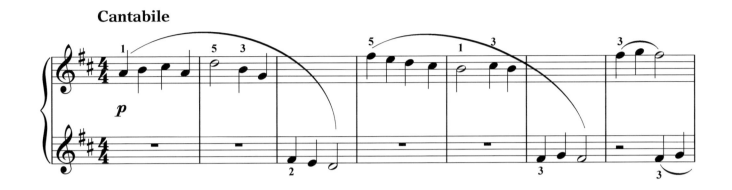

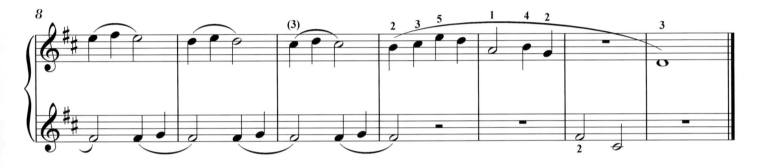

4
At Recess

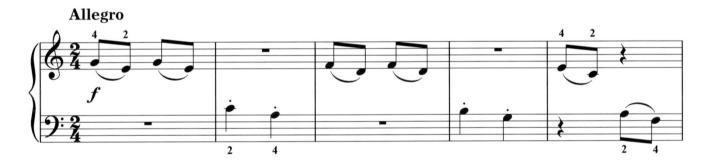

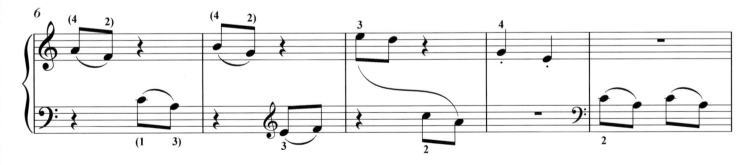

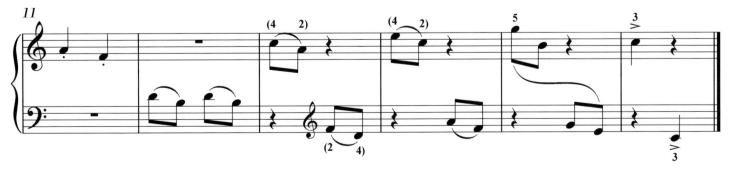

4

5
First Waltz

Non allegro

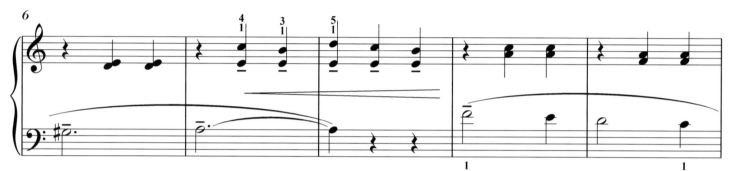

6
The Jumping Champion

Marcato

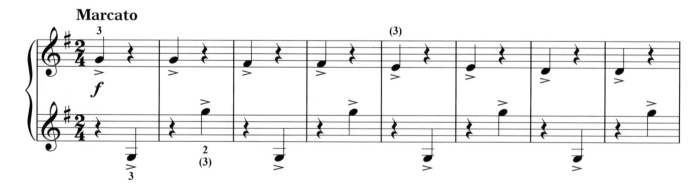

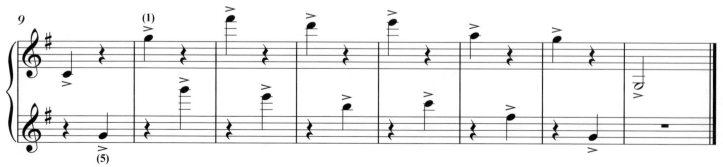

7
Light and Shadow

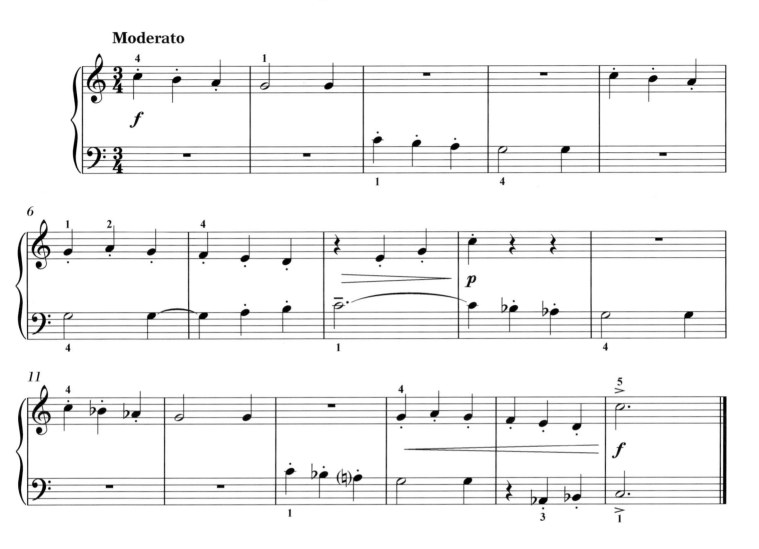

8
Little Hedgehog

6

9
Song in Octaves

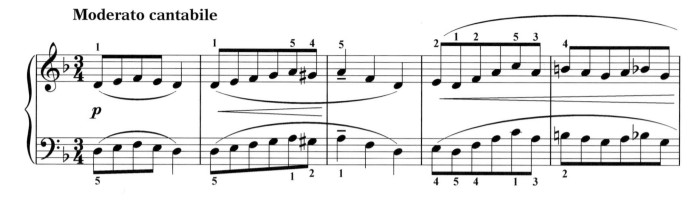

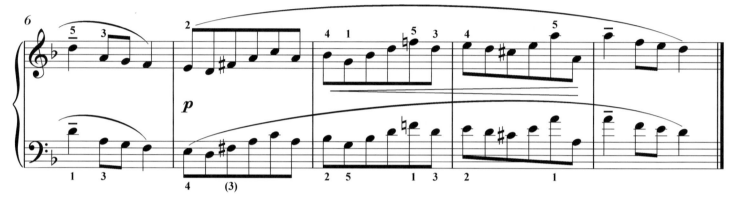

10
Playful One

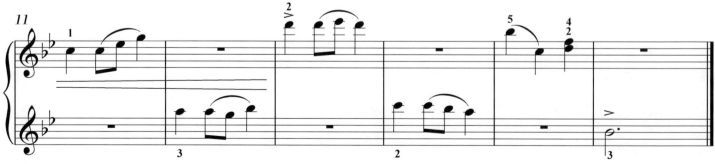

11
Crybaby

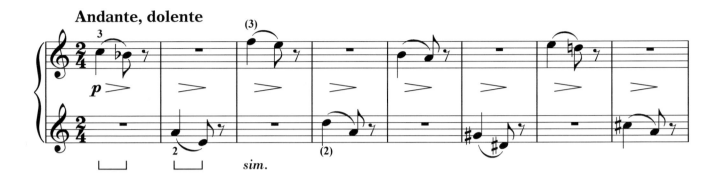

12
The Shrew

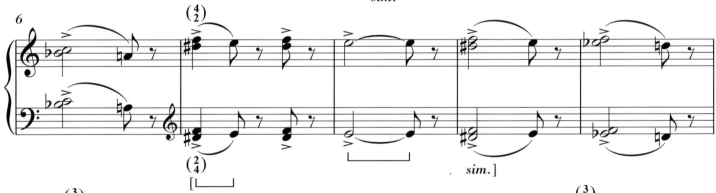

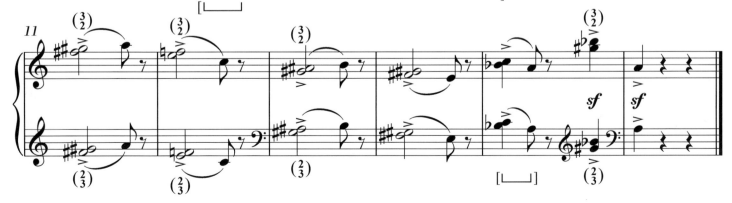

13
Soothing Song

14
Morning Song

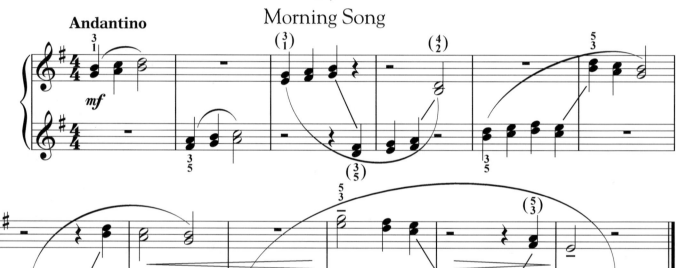

15
Trumpet and Echo

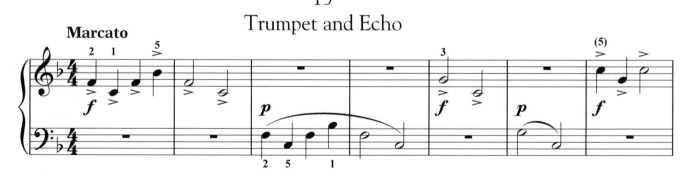

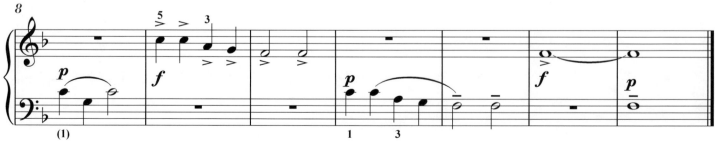

16
Evening Song

Andante cantabile

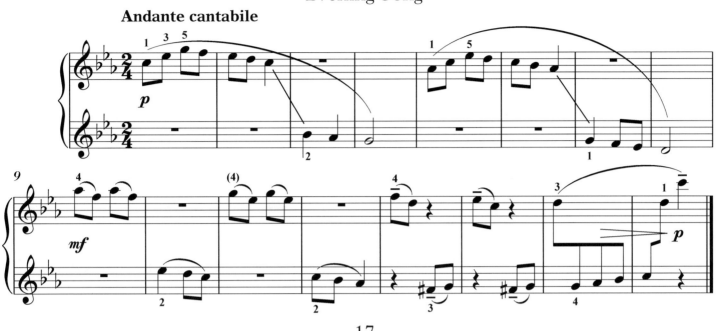

17
Skipping Rope

Happily

accel. poco a poco al fine

18
On the Ice

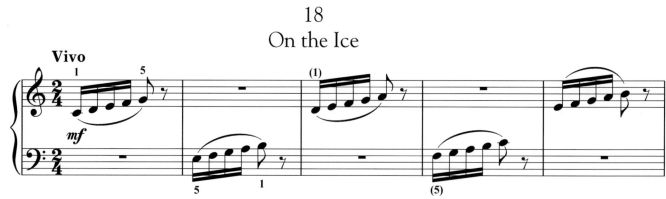

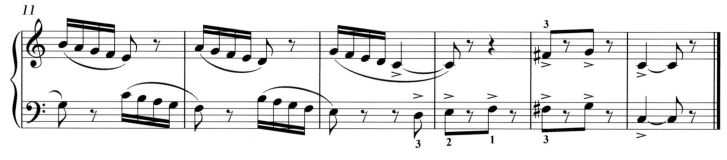

19
Little Goat Limping

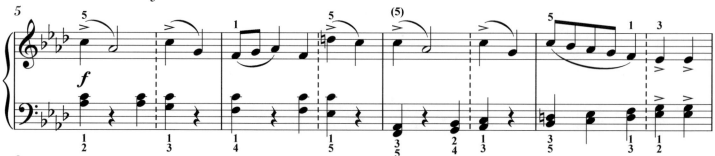

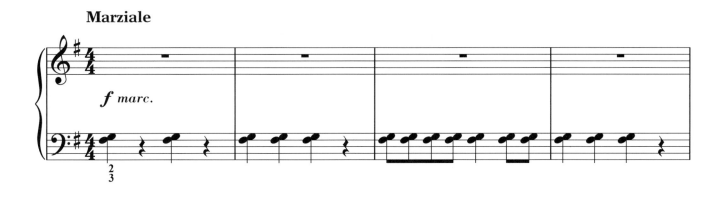

20
Trumpet and Drum

21
The Little Juggler

22
March

23
Brave Song

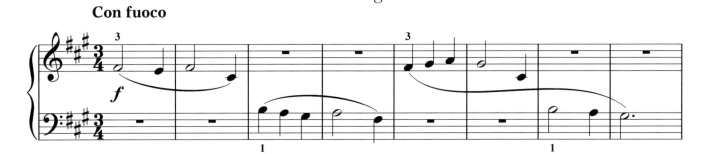

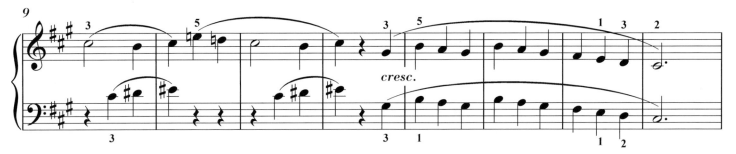

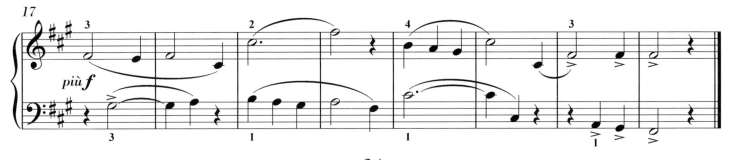

24
The Little Harpist

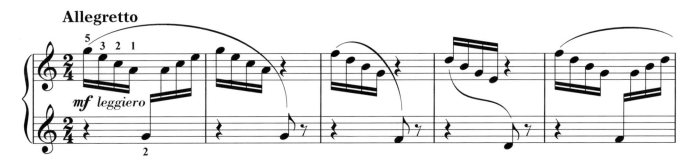

25
Chastushka

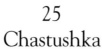

Scherzando

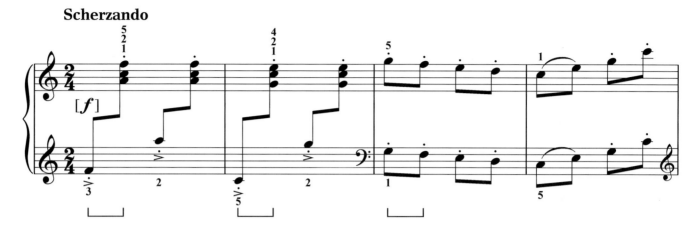

A *chastushka* is a short, lighthearted, satirical verse in Russian, similar to a limerick in English.

26
A Merry Game

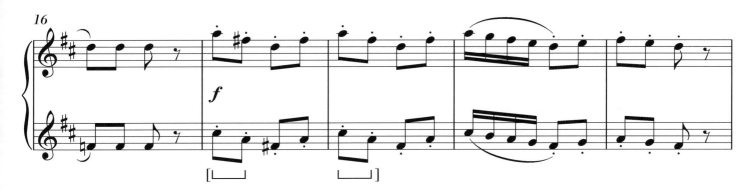

27
Stubborn Little Brother

*Use fingers 2 and 3.

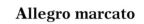

28
Buratino's Dance

Allegro marcato

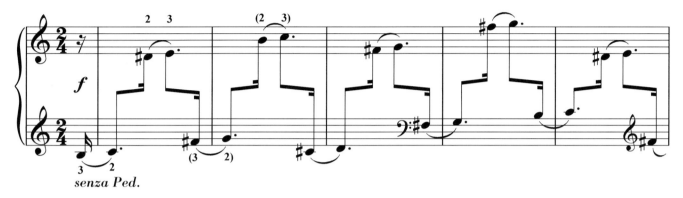

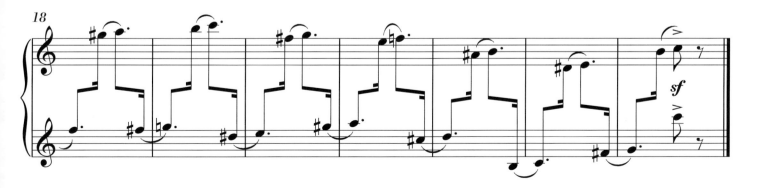

29
Melody

Tranquillo, cantabile

mp

tenuto con ped.

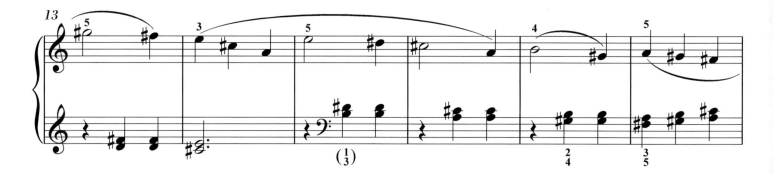

mf

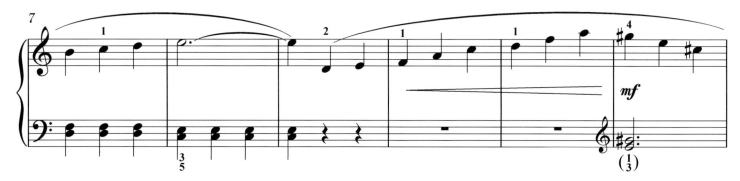

dim.

p

poco rit.

30
Fighting Song

Energico

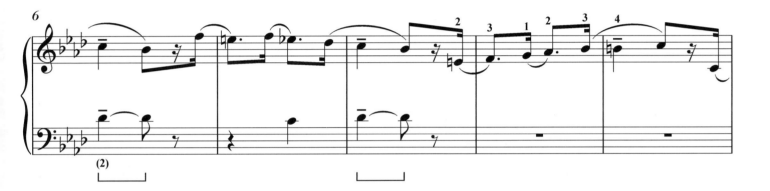

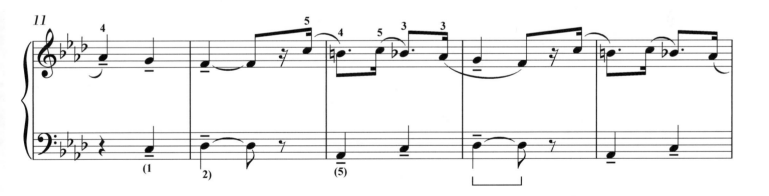

31
Rabbit Teasing a Bear-Cub

Allegretto

32
Little Hippo Dance

Andante pesante

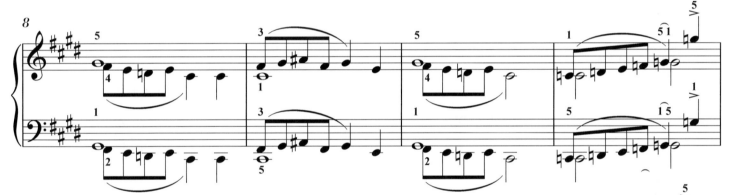

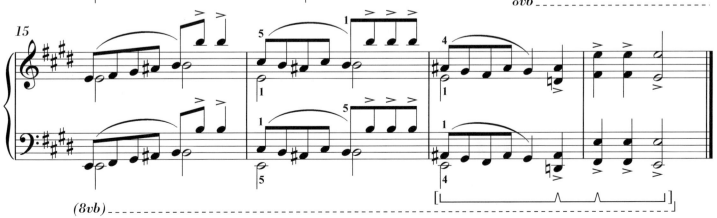

33
Almost a Waltz

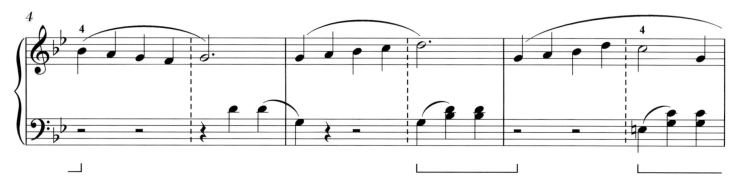

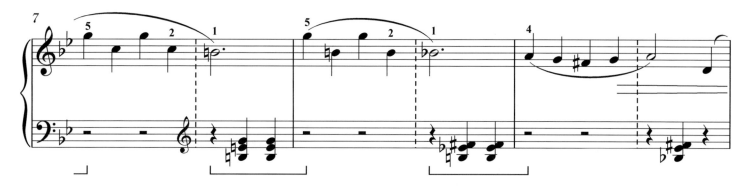

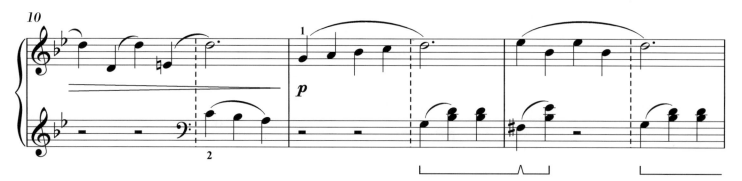

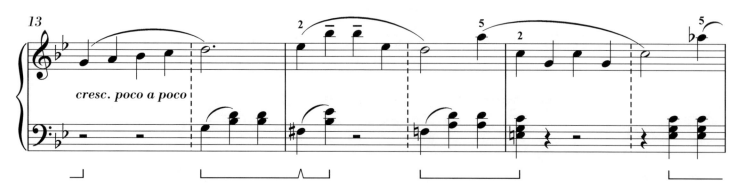

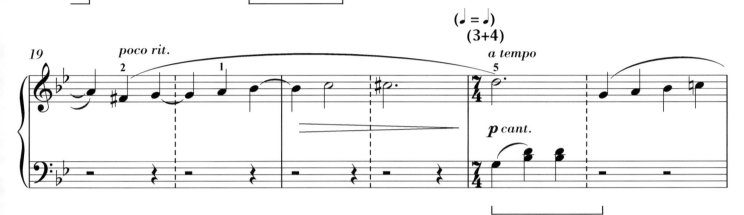

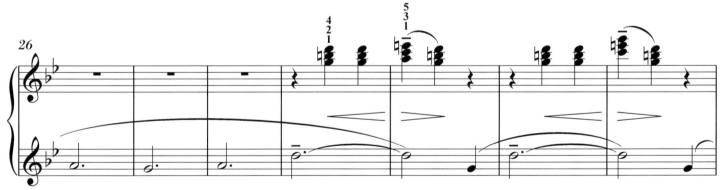

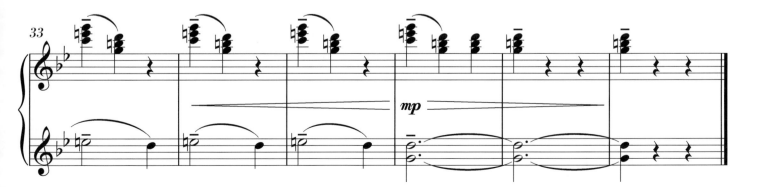

34
Melancholy Rain

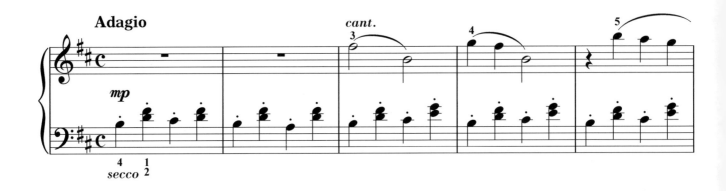

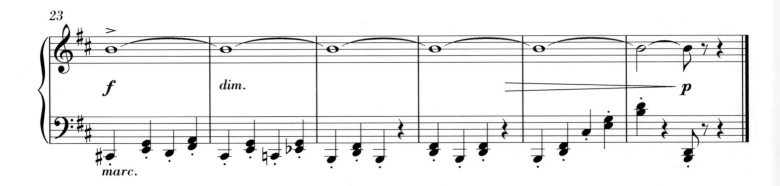

35
By the Water

ABOUT THE EDITOR

RICHARD WALTERS

Richard Walters is a pianist, composer, and editor of hundred of publications in a long music publishing career. He is Vice President of Classical Publications at Hal Leonard, and directs a variety of publications for piano, voice, and solo instruments. Walters directs all publishing in the Schirmer Performance Editions series. Among other piano publications, he is editor of the revised edition of *Samuel Barber: Complete Piano Music*, *Leonard Bernstein: Music for Piano*, and the multi-volume series *The World's Great Classical Music*. His editing credits for vocal publications include *Samuel Barber: 65 Songs*, *Benjamin Britten: Collected Songs*, *Benjamin Britten: Complete Folksong Arrangements*, *Leonard Bernstein: Art Songs and Arias*, *The Purcell Collection: Realizations by Benjamin Britten*, *Bernstein Theatre Songs*, *G. Schirmer Collection of American Art Song*, *28 Italian Songs and Arias for the Seventeenth and Eighteenth Centuries*, 80 volumes of standard repertoire in the Vocal Library series, and the multi-volume *The Singer's Musical Theatre Anthology*. Walters has published dozens of various arrangements, particularly for voice and piano, and is the composer of nine song cycles. He was educated with a bachelor's degree in piano at Simpson College, where he studied piano with Robert Larsen and composition with Sven Lekberg, and graduate studies in composition at the University of Minnesota, where he studied with Dominick Argento.